CANADA
the land

Bobbie Kalman

The Lands, Peoples, and Cultures Series

Crabtree Publishing Company

The Lands, Peoples, and Cultures Series

Created by Bobbie Kalman

Editor-in-chief
Bobbie Kalman

Writing team
Bobbie Kalman
Janine Schaub
David Schimpky

Editors
David Schimpky
Lynda Hale

Research
Janine Schaub

Design and computer layout
Antoinette "Cookie" DeBiasi

Cover mechanicals and maps
Rose Campbell

Illustrations
Antoinette "Cookie" DeBiasi

Art on title page
Courtesy of the Weir Collection,
Queenston, Ontario: "Meadow Stream
in Early Winter" by Maurice Cullen

Printer
Worzalla Publishing Company

Separations and film
Kedia Inc.

For Kate and Mike Belec

Special thanks to: Theatre Beyond Words, Halifax Tourism, Health and Welfare Canada, Imperial Oil Limited, Industry, Science, and Technology Canada, The Ontario Ministry of Tourism and Recreation, James Campbell and the Weir Foundation, Union Gas Limited

Photographs

Marc Crabtree: page 15 (top)
Ken Faris: page 11
Halifax Tourism: page 23
Health and Welfare Canada: pages 7 (bottom), 25 (top)
Imperial Oil Limited: page 15 (second from bottom)
Industry, Science, and Technology Canada: cover, pages 3, 7 (middle), 8 (right), 13 (middle), 14 (inset), 15 (second from top), 16 (bottom), 17 (both), 18, 19 (bottom right, bottom left), 23 (inset), 25 (middle right, bottom left), 27 (top), 29 (bottom), 30
Peter Crabtree: pages 19 (top left), 20 (bottom), 25 (bottom right)
James Kamstra: pages 7 (top), 13 (top, bottom left), 14, 27 (bottom right), 29 (top)
Diane Payton Majumdar: pages 10, 13 (bottom right), 19 (top right), 21
Ontario Ministry of Tourism and Recreation: pages 4, 9 (both), 20 (top), 22
Rudy Schimpky: page 12
Dave Taylor: pages 26, 27 (bottom left)
Theatre Beyond Words: page 16 (top)
Union Gas Limited/Dan Spencer: page 15 (bottom)
Wally Worden: page 8 (both inset)

Published by
Crabtree Publishing Company

350 Fifth Avenue
Suite 3308
New York
N.Y. 10118

360 York Road, RR 4,
Niagara-on-the-Lake,
Ontario, Canada
L0S 1J0

73 Lime Walk
Headington
Oxford OX3 7AD
United Kingdom

Cataloguing in Publication Data

Kalman, Bobbie, 1947-
  Canada: the land

(Lands, Peoples, and Cultures Series)
Includes index.
ISBN 0-86505-217-4 (library bound) ISBN 0-86505-297-2 (pbk.)
This book examines geography, resources, industry, and transportation in Canada.

1. Canada - Description and travel - Juvenile literature.
I. Title. II. Series.

FC75.K35 1993   j971   LC 93-23516
F1017.K35 1993

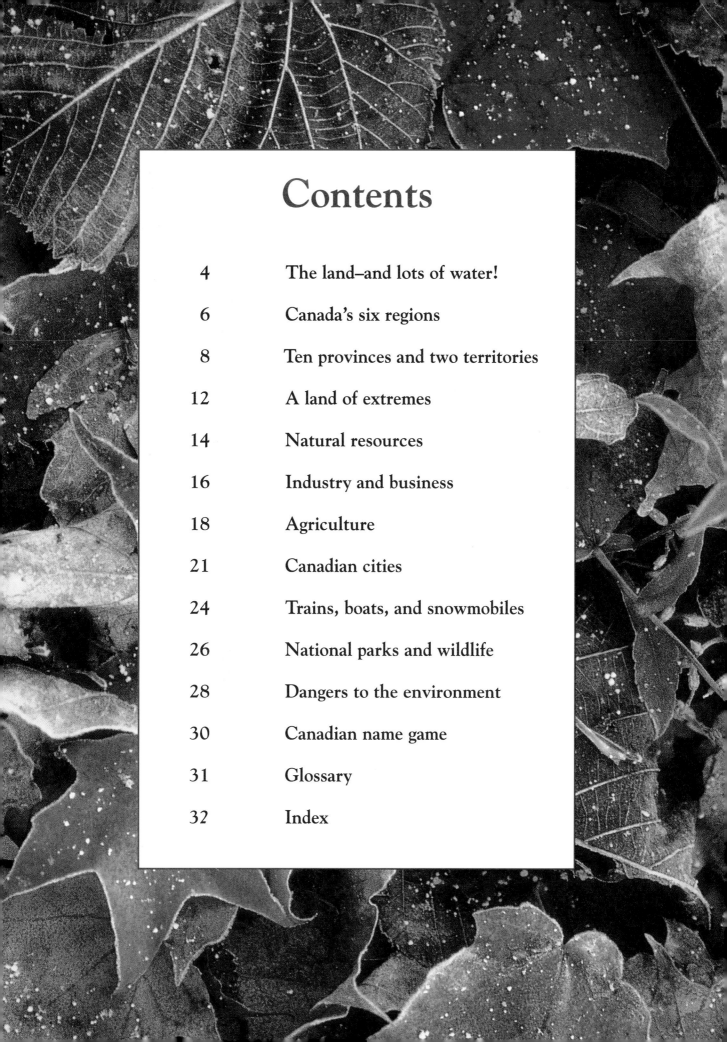

Contents

🍁 The land–and lots of water! 🍁

What pops into your mind when you hear the name "Canada?" To some people, it may suggest images of snow-capped mountains, open grasslands, and dense forests. To others, Canada means bustling cities, busy highways, and a wealth of natural resources such as trees, oil, and natural gas.

Not many people would think of water when they think of Canada, but water makes up much of the country's area. The national motto "from sea to sea" describes a land that stretches from the Atlantic to the Pacific and north to the Arctic Ocean. In-between, Canada is dotted with millions of freshwater lakes that are connected to one another by rivers and streams. Half of the fresh water in the world can be found in Canada!

Glaciers carved the landscape of the Canadian Shield, which covers much of Canada. Most of the Shield is blanketed by forests. In autumn, the trees turn spectacular colors.

The work of the glaciers

Frozen water was responsible for shaping the Canadian landscape. Thousands of years ago most of Canada was covered by huge rivers of ice called **glaciers**. Like giant bulldozers, the glaciers pushed and carved the land beneath them. When the glaciers melted, they left behind hills, valleys, and ridges. Holes in the earth were filled with meltwater, creating glacial lakes. Gullies became rivers. Over the centuries, plants, animals, and people made this rugged land their home.

A resource of great value

In the past, waterways of Canada were of great value to both the Native peoples and the European settlers because traveling by water was the easiest way to get from place to place. Today the water systems are just as important. The St. Lawrence and the Great Lakes are still used for shipping, and the swift-flowing rivers provide electricity for homes and industries.

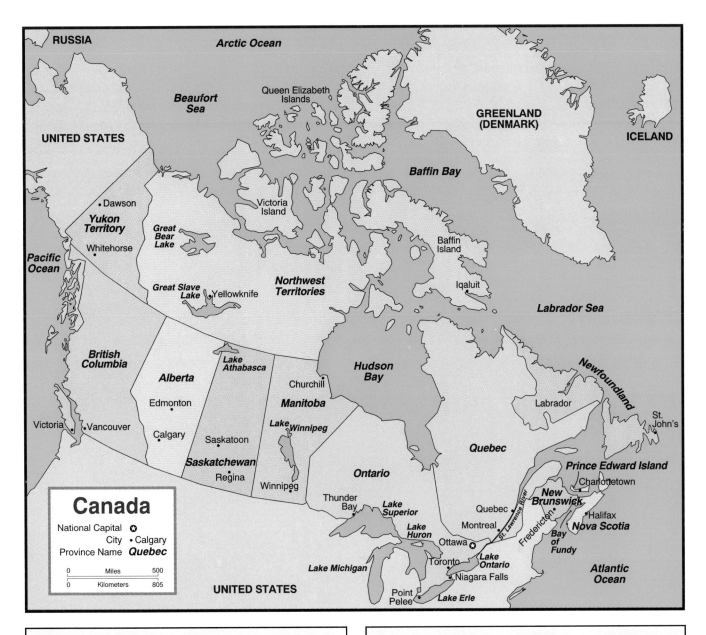

Canada

National Capital	✪
City	• Calgary
Province Name	*Quebec*

	Miles	
0		500
0	Kilometers	805

Facts at a glance

Area: 9, 970, 610 km² (3,849,954 square miles)

Canada is the second-largest country in the world.

Population: 27,000,000

Currency: Canadian dollar (100 cents)

National symbols: Maple leaf and beaver

Official languages: English and French

Canada's capitals

The capital city of Canada is Ottawa.

Provinces	Capital cities
British Columbia	Victoria
Alberta	Edmonton
Saskatchewan	Regina
Manitoba	Winnipeg
Ontario	Toronto
Quebec	Quebec City
New Brunswick	Fredericton
Nova Scotia	Halifax
Prince Edward Island	Charlottetown
Newfoundland	St. John's

Territories

Northwest Territories	Yellowknife
Yukon	Whitehorse

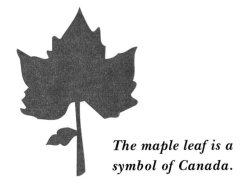

The maple leaf is a symbol of Canada.

Arctic Ocean

Pacific Ocean

Atlantic Ocean

🍁 Canada's six regions 🍁

Although Canada is divided into ten provinces and two northern territories, it is easier to describe the land by its six geographical regions:

1. The Atlantic Region
2. The Canadian Shield
3. The Great Lakes–St. Lawrence Lowlands
4. The Interior Plains
5. The Cordillera
6. The Arctic

The Atlantic Region
The Atlantic Region is a mixture of rocky shorelines, sandy beaches, rich farmland, and thick forests. The provinces of New Brunswick, Nova Scotia, Prince Edward Island, and the island

part of the province of Newfoundland belong to this region. These provinces are also called the **Maritimes**, a word meaning "on or near the sea."

The Canadian Shield
The Canadian Shield is a rocky land mass that covers nearly half of Canada. It is one of the earth's oldest landforms. If you visited the Canadian Shield and picked up one of its pinkish stones, you could be holding a 600-million-year-old mineral in your hand! This hard rock is called **granite**, and it reaches far below the surface of the earth. The landscape of the Canadian Shield consists of bare rock, thick forests, and cold freshwater lakes (see picture on page 4).

The Lowlands

The Great Lakes–St. Lawrence Lowlands are located between the Canadian Shield and the north shores of Lake Ontario, Lake Erie, and the banks of the St. Lawrence River. This narrow area of level land is home to two-thirds of the country's population and produces three-quarters of the country's manufactured goods. With its fertile farmland and many industries, this region is often referred to as "Canada's heartland."

The Interior Plains

Flat grasslands and gently rolling hills are familiar sights across the Interior Plains, or **prairie**, region of Canada. The plains stretch over the provinces of Manitoba, Saskatchewan, and Alberta. This region is famous for grain farming and cattle ranching. It also contains a wealth of natural resources such as minerals, oil, and natural gas.

The Cordillera

As you head further west, the gentle landscape of the prairie suddenly rises to meet the Rocky Mountains. Jagged, snow-capped peaks run north-south through the Yukon, western Alberta, and British Columbia, forming the region called the **Cordillera**. The Cordillera area boasts coastal forests with thousand-year-old gigantic trees and southern valleys that are ideal for growing fruit. Most of the people who make the Cordillera their home live in the south-western corner of British Columbia, in or near the city of Vancouver.

The Arctic

"The sun shines at midnight and millions of tiny wildflowers bloom next to sparkling ponds," describes the short summer in the far northern region of the Arctic. During the long, dark winter, snow blows across the mountains, frozen oceans, and the desert-like area known as the **tundra**. The northern part of the Arctic is an **archipelago**, or a group of islands. These islands, which are located in the Arctic Ocean, are the world's largest archipelago.

(above) The Great Lakes-St. Lawrence Lowlands are ideal for farming. Holland Marsh is a fertile lowland area north of Toronto.

(above) The Plains in the foreground and the mountains of the Cordillera are both evident in this Alberta picture. (below) Winter is cold and windy in the Arctic. The sun shines only a few hours each day.

Ten provinces and two territories

Canada is the second-largest country in the world. It has ten provinces, two northern territories, and a great variety of landscapes.

Friendly Newfoundland

The province of Newfoundland is made up of a mainland area and a large island. The mainland section is called Labrador. Labrador is part of the Canadian Shield, except its northern area, which is barren and arctic-like. The island of Newfoundland is a quiet, friendly place. Most of its residents live on the coast because fishing is the main occupation.

Peaceful Prince Edward Island

Canada's smallest province is Prince Edward Island. Many farmers have settled in this area because the warm climate and rich soil are well suited for growing a variety of fruits and vegetables. Sandstone cliffs, green fields, sandy white beaches, and gentle hills can be found throughout this picturesque province.

Scenic Nova Scotia

Nova Scotia means "New Scotland," and the province looks a lot like the country after which it was named. Misty highlands, flower-filled valleys, winding rivers, and old villages are all part of the landscape. Cape Breton Island is part of this province. Its scenic Cabot Trail highway winds through the island.

High tides off New Brunswick

Forests cover ninety percent of New Brunswick. The rest of the countryside is a combination of mountains, plains, marshes, and rugged coastline. The Bay of Fundy is a large inlet that separates New Brunswick from Nova Scotia. It has the world's largest tides. The water level can rise 16 meters (52 feet). At low tide you can stand on the tidal flats but, at high tide, you would have to wear stilts four-stories tall to avoid the rising water! The location, shape, and size of the bay are all responsible for the powerful tides.

The tide is in at the Bay of Fundy.

Tide's out!

Quaint Quebec

Quebec is Canada's largest province. It is three times as big as France! Quebec has fertile farmlands, great coniferous forests, and picturesque mountains. The mighty St. Lawrence River connects the province to the sea. The countryside reminds people of Europe. The houses have colorful roofs, and there are many beautiful churches. More than 90 percent of the French-Canadian population lives in Quebec.

Amazing Ontario

Ontario is Canada's second-largest province, but it is the wealthiest and most populated. Its name, which means "beautiful water," suits this province because lakes and rivers occupy almost one-fifth of its area. Northern Ontario belongs to the Canadian Shield, whereas most of southern Ontario is part of the lowlands. Cities, farms, industries, and 90 percent of the population can be found in the lowland area.

Ontario has some magnificent sights. Niagara Falls, one of the world's seven natural wonders, is located on its southern border. Niagara's thundering water drops 54 meters (176 feet)!

Point Pelee

Point Pelee is a small peninsula in Ontario that juts out into Lake Erie at the southernmost tip of mainland Canada. It is as far south as northern California. Plant and animal species that cannot live in colder parts of the country can be found there. Over 300 species of migrating birds stop at Point Pelee after their long flight across Lake Erie. This unique peninsula has been made into a national park.

At Tobermory, on the shoreline of Georgian Bay, there are strange-looking landforms called flowerpots. *The bases of these tall rock formations have been worn away by wind and water. The wide top is capped with small trees, shrubs, and flowers, just like a flowerpot!*

Alberta and British Columbia share the Rocky Mountains, one of Canada's spectacular wilderness areas.

Manitoba's variety

Open grasslands dominate the south of Manitoba, forests are in the middle, and bush and tundra cover the northern part of the province. The climate of this province ranges from arctic-like winters to warm summers. Half the population lives in the capital city of Winnipeg, which is known for its multicultural festivals.

Huge farms in Saskatchewan

The name of this province comes from a Cree word meaning "swiftly flowing river." Saskatchewan has, indeed, many rivers and lakes. It also has rocky areas, forests, and huge stretches of prairie farmland. The grain farms in Saskatchewan are so big that they make other farms look like postage stamps. The grain is stored in huge, colorful elevators that can be seen great distances away. It is shipped all over the world.

Breathtaking Alberta

Alberta is a great place to live! Not only is it the sunniest province in Canada, but it has magnificent mountains, golden prairies, exciting cities and untouched wilderness. Saskatchewan and Alberta share the **badlands**, a barren area with strange rock formations called **hoodoos**. This area holds some of the world's richest deposits of fossils and dinosaur bones.

Beautiful British Columbia

British Columbia is known as "Canada's playground." Most of the province is covered by forests and mountains. The Okanagan Valley offers orchards filled with delicious apples, apricots, peaches, cherries, and grapes. Vancouver has the world's largest city park, Stanley Park, which features hiking trails, a zoo, an aquarium, and beaches.

Rainforests in Canada?

Few people are aware that Canada is home to rainforests as spectacular as those in the Amazon region of South America. The rainforests are located on the coast of British Columbia, the Queen Charlotte Islands, and Vancouver Island. The forests have developed during thousands of years of mild weather and abundant rainfall. A rich undergrowth of mosses, ferns, and flowers are sheltered by the canopies of enormous trees such as the Sitka spruce and Douglas fir. The lush rainforest is home to many animal species such as the cougar, bald eagle, and marmot.

Canada's north

There are two territories in Canada's north: the Yukon and Northwest Territories. The Northwest Territories will be divided in 1999 and one portion, called **Nunavut**, will be governed by Native residents.

Canada's northern territories have **permafrost**. Permafrost is soil that is always frozen. Only the thin top layer of the earth thaws during the summer. Permafrost prevents certain kinds of plants from growing. Trees, for example, do not survive in permafrost because their roots can not grow down into the frozen earth.

Anyone for pingo?

What looks like a volcano but has a core of ice? If you said an Arctic pingo, you would be right! Pingos are huge domes of soil and ice. A pingo is formed when a small frozen lake is covered by a thin layer of soil. The lake water freezes under the soil, expanding upward to form a hill on the land. The earth that covers the pingo prevents the ice underneath from melting. At the top of the pingo the soil is easily blown off by the wind. When the sun shines, the uncovered ice melts and leaves a depression. This depression looks like the hole, or **crater**, of a volcano.

Most pingos are found around the mouth of the Mackenzie River. They are thousands of years old.

🍁 A land of extremes 🍁

On the same day that a person in southern Ontario is experiencing a sizzling 30°C (86°F) afternoon, someone in the Arctic may still be playing in the snow. Canada is such an enormous land that extreme differences in weather conditions are not unusual. Canada's climate, however, is not as cold as many people think. Most Canadians live in areas with **temperate** conditions. The freezing winter is followed by a mild spring, hot summer, and cool fall. People adjust to the changing temperatures and enjoy the beauty of each season.

Bursting with color

After months of winter, spring arrives with a burst of color. The grass emerges from beneath the snow, and buds and blossoms appear on the trees. Blue, yellow, and white spring flowers display their early blooms.

In September and October, Canada's vast forests turn brilliant shades of yellow, orange, and red. Even in the treeless Arctic, small shrubs, mosses, and leafy plants change from burgundy red to golden yellow.

Be prepared

Canada's climate often brings surprising changes in the weather. A warm wind called a **chinook** can melt a prairie snow cover in just a few hours. Thick Maritime fog moves quickly into a harbor and makes it nearly impossible to see a fishing pole in your hands. Hailstones as big as marbles sometimes fall during the summer, damaging farmers' crops in minutes. A warm spring day in the Rocky Mountains lures skiers in T-shirts and shorts to the bright, sunny slopes. The scout motto "be prepared" has special meaning for Canadian boys and girls!

(top) Going to the beach is a great way to keep cool in the hot summer. (right) On a cold winter day, it is wise to bundle up to avoid a "froze" nose. (bottom right) The crocus is the first spring flower to poke its blooms out from under the snow. (bottom left) Maple trees turn beautiful shades of orange and red in the autumn.

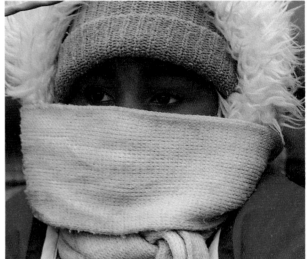

Natural resources

Canada is famous for its wealth of natural resources. Trees, animals, water, minerals, and fuels are examples of raw materials that have been harvested, hunted, and mined for centuries.

Living off the land

There are two kinds of natural resources. Water, plants, animals, and fish are **renewable resources**. They can be used and replaced; new trees grow, more animals are born, and rain falls to fill rivers. Some of these resources, however, such as huge trees, take hundreds of years to grow to full size.

Substances that are mined from the earth, such as minerals, oil, and natural gas, are **non-renewable resources**. Once these resources are removed, they can not be replaced for millions of years. Some people still believe that there are enough Canadian resources to last forever. Unfortunately, many natural resources have already been wasted.

(above) Trees blanket almost half of Canada. Forests supply lumber, paper, and wood for fuel. (inset) The city of Sudbury, Ontario, is famous for nickel mining. Coal, zinc, copper, and iron are also mined in Canada.

Not long ago fish swam in great numbers in Canada's many waterways. Over-fishing by Canadian and foreign boats has greatly reduced the natural abundance of fish. Fish markets throughout Canada are still, however, filled with food from the sea such as lobster, shrimp, cod, mackerel, halibut, and salmon.

Water power

With so many swift-flowing rivers, it is not surprising that **hydroelectricity** is one of Canada's main sources of power. Hydroelectric power is created when water spins a turbine. Many people are in favor of this type of energy because it does not pollute the environment. The picture on the right shows a hydroelectric dam.

Oil from the ground and sea

Oil is needed to run cars, trucks, and planes. It is also used to make asphalt and plastics. Most of Canada's crude oil, or **petroleum**, comes from large deposits in Alberta and Saskatchewan. Oil can also be found in the Arctic and in Canada's coastal waters. This picture shows an oil well drilled deep into the northern earth!

Natural gas

Natural gas is a colorless, odorless fossil fuel found under the earth. When burned, it creates less pollution than oil or coal. Most of Canada's natural gas comes from Alberta and is distributed by a huge system of pipelines across Canada and the United States. The photograph on the right shows a natural-gas pipeline being built.

Industry and business

(above) Entertainment is part of the service industry. This picture shows a production of "The Potato People," which was performed by Theatre Beyond Words in Niagara-on-the-Lake, Ontario.

(below) Car manufacturing depends on a ready supply of steel and electricity. Canada has both.

Some of Canada's industries depend on the country's abundant natural resources. Industries that gather and sell natural resources are called **primary industries**. Industries that make goods from these raw materials are called **secondary industries**. The two industries rely on each other for business.

One example of a secondary industry that depends on a primary industry is car manufacturing. Cars are made from steel, and Canada is one of the world's largest producers of this metal. Iron ore, the raw material from which steel is made, is mined from rich deposits in Quebec, Labrador, and British Columbia. Most iron and steel manufacturing takes place in Ontario.

To take advantage of the plentiful supply of steel and electricity, automobile companies from all over the world have built factories in Canada. The auto industry provides jobs for many Canadians. Most are employed by the three largest American companies: General Motors, Ford, and Chrysler.

Service with a smile

Canada's largest industry is the **service industry**. Its business is helping people. Banks, accounting firms, supermarkets, and health clubs all offer services to people. Some of these organizations are privately owned, and others are operated by the government.

Canadians and millions of foreign tourists depend on the service industry. Tourists spend money in hotels, restaurants, theaters, shops, amusement parks, and on taxis. This money helps pay the salaries of thousands of Canadians who work in the service industry.

Services in your community

Which services did you use this week? Did you know that school is a service? Your doctor, dentist, library, hospital, church or temple, gas station, post office, and school bus are other services offered by most communities.

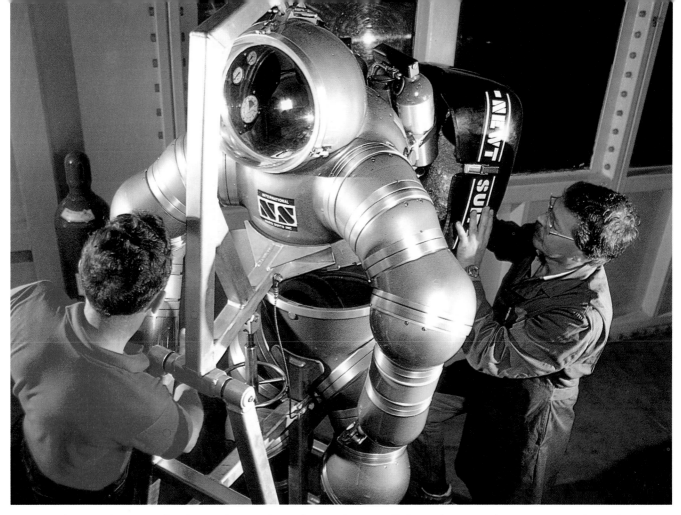

Canada is a world leader in high-tech manufacturing. This hard diving suit was designed by Canadian scientists. It allows divers to explore the deepest parts of the ocean. Computers, satellites, and countless other modern devices are also made in Canada.

Is free trade a good idea?

To make money, Canada's companies depend on selling their goods in other countries. Other countries also sell goods in Canada. This exchange of goods is called **trade**. Canada trades most of its products with the United States. To make trade easier between these countries, the two governments have signed a **free-trade pact**. This agreement means that special taxes, called **duties**, will not be placed on Canadian goods sold in the United States or vice versa.

Many Canadians feel that this agreement has hurt Canada because people prefer to buy less-expensive American products instead of higher-priced Canadian products. Other people, however, believe that free trade will eventually provide more business for Canadian companies.

(above) Pulp and paper manufacturing is one of Canada's largest industries. It relies on forestry (a primary industry) for its raw materials. Most pulp and paper mills are located in British Columbia, Ontario, and Quebec.

17

🍁 Agriculture 🍁

Farming took place in Canada thousands of years ago. Although most of the Native peoples lived **nomadic** lives, some stayed in one place and farmed the land. They grew corn, beans, and squash and harvested wild rice. In later years they traded their extra produce with the new settlers from Europe. Immigrants who came to Canada slowly cut down the huge forests that covered most of the countryside and cleared the land of stumps and rocks. They began to raise livestock and grow a variety of crops.

Specialized farming
Just one hundred years ago, seven out of every ten Canadian families worked in agriculture. Their farms included both crops and livestock. Today only one or two families in a hundred are farmers. To save money, most farmers concentrate on raising one crop or one type of livestock. A farm in the prairies may grow only wheat, whereas another farm in Quebec may concentrate on raising beef cattle. This type of farming is called **specialized farming**.

(right) Some farms specialize in raising dairy cows. Using modern equipment, the cows are milked each day. Cheese, sour cream, and yogurt are just a few products made from milk—and milk is enjoyed just on its own, of course.

(left) These pumpkins are for sale at an Ontario fruit stand. They might be carved into jack o'lanterns at Hallowe'en or become delicious pumpkin pies for Thanksgiving dinner.

(right) One of Canada's more popular fruits is the apple. Juicy red apples are picked from trees in the early autumn. Canadians love to drink apple cider, which is made by pressing apples in a machine to make the juice come out. Some people drink hot cider spiced with cinnamon and cloves.

(left) In the early summer, children and adults gather to pick strawberries from the fields.

(opposite page) Beautiful yellow rapeseed fields can be found in the prairies. A vegetable oil called canola oil is made from rapeseed. It is very good for your health!

(above) Ottawa's parliament buildings can be seen in the distance, behind the Rideau Canal.
(below) Tourists love the old historic part of Quebec City.

Canadian cities

Canada has very few large cities, but they are popular places to live. Most Canadians reside in or around urban centers. About one-third of Canada's population is concentrated in the country's three largest cities: Toronto, Montreal, and Vancouver.

Ottawa, the unlikely capital

In the early nineteenth century, Ottawa was a small logging settlement called Bytown. Its present name comes from an Algonquin word meaning "a place of buying and selling." Queen Victoria surprised her subjects by choosing this city as Canada's capital. Today Ottawa is not a large city, but it is a beautiful one. The Rideau Canal winds through the heart of town, past parks and historic buildings. In the winter, the canal becomes the world's longest skating rink!

Historic Quebec City

Settled in 1608, Quebec City is one of Canada's oldest cities and Quebec's capital. It is the only walled city in Canada. Visiting Quebec City is like walking into a fairy-tale town. In the historic section, narrow cobblestone streets are lined with colorfully painted shop fronts. Artists, jugglers, and street musicians show off their talents to interested tourists. A large castle-like hotel called the Château Frontenac dominates the city. Outside the city walls is the newer part of town, where most of the residents live.

Beautiful Vancouver

Can you imagine spending the day downhill skiing in the mountains and the evening windsurfing on the beach? You can do these things and many more in Vancouver! With the Pacific coast on one side and the Coast Mountains on the other, Vancouver is surrounded by beauty. Its magnificent views and spectacular parks attract many tourists. Vancouver is bordered by a warm ocean, making it one of Canada's warmest and wettest cities. The city and surrounding areas receive a lot of rain because the clouds that roll in from over the ocean break up when they reach the mountains.

Vancouver is on the west coast of Canada. It has mountains, beautiful parks, and an ocean view.

Bustling Toronto

With a population of over three-and-a-half million people, Toronto is Canada's biggest city and Ontario's capital. If you look at the jagged skyline reflected peacefully in Lake Ontario, you might not believe that the downtown area is bustling with activity. Toronto may be all business by day but, in the evening, it offers a wonderful variety of cultural activities such as music, art, dance, and theater. Two famous Canadian structures, the CN Tower and the Skydome, are in Toronto. The former is the largest free-standing structure in the world. The latter is a sports complex with a top that opens and closes.

Popular Montreal

Montreal is in the province of Quebec. It is Canada's second-largest city and the second-largest French-speaking city in the world. The old part of town is located on an island in the St. Lawrence River on top of an extinct volcano called Mount Royal. Montreal has grown beyond its island setting and has become an interesting blend of old and new architecture. Tourists enjoy strolling along streets lined with outdoor cafés.

Halifax, a harbor city

Halifax, the capital of Nova Scotia, is located on an inlet of the Atlantic Ocean. The city was founded in 1749 by British settlers and was an important military base for many years. A fortress called the "Halifax Citadel" was built high on a hill to protect the city. Today, Halifax's ice-free harbor is one of the busiest in Canada, exporting fish, lumber, and agricultural products. Halifax is also home to six universities, two colleges, many churches, and historic parks.

(opposite page) Toronto is visited by millions of tourists each year. It is a clean, safe, and exciting city. (inset) Montreal is famous for its yearly jazz festival. (bottom) Many great tall ships were built in Halifax. The boat in the picture is a replica of the Bluenose, the schooner featured on the Canadian dime.

Trains, boats, and snowmobiles

Before the invention of automobiles, airplanes, and railways, traveling across the land in Canada was extremely difficult because there were a lot of trees and no roads. The Native peoples took advantage of rivers and lakes to make canoe voyages. In the north, the Inuit used dog sleds to travel over the snow. Early Europeans brought horses and sailing ships, but getting from place to place still took a long time.

The national dream

At the beginning of the nineteenth century the steam engine was invented. It was used to power boats and trains. Trains changed the way people traveled. Distances that once took weeks to cover now took just a few days. Many Canadians were eager to have a railroad built to connect the east with the west. The idea of building a railroad right across the country was called "the national dream." Sir John A. Macdonald, Canada's first Prime Minister, made it his most important project, but it was not an easy task. The builders had to cut through the rugged Canadian Shield and the towering mountains of the Cordillera. Workers built huge bridges across valleys and blasted long tunnels out of the rock. In 1885 the railway was finally completed. The train played an important role in uniting Canada.

Modern rail travel

Today the Canadian government owns and operates most of the trains that travel the country's 100,000 kilometers (62,000 miles) of track. Recently, passenger service has been reduced to help the government save money. The train no longer stops in some towns that have had rail service for over a century.

Shipping

Canada still relies on ships to carry goods across the country and around the world. Canada's major ports are Vancouver, Churchill, Montreal, Quebec City, Halifax, and St. John's. The St. Lawrence Seaway allows ocean-going ships to enter into the heart of the country. It is 3862 kilometers (2400 miles) long and has twenty-six locks and five canals.

A very long highway

Traveling by car is the most popular method of getting around in Canada. A highly developed system of roads carries Canada's nearly twelve million cars. The Trans-Canada Highway is the longest paved highway in the world. It extends 7500 kilometers (4660 miles) from St. John's, Newfoundland to Victoria, British Columbia.

One Canadian's doo-ing

One man's vision resulted in an invention that has changed the lives of many. The dream was to create a vehicle that could travel on snow. Born in Quebec in 1908, J. Armand Bombardier spent his young adult years developing what he would call the **Ski-doo**, or snowmobile. In 1937 he created the first models, which were quite large and carried a number of passengers. These early snowmobiles were used mainly as medical vehicles. Today Ski-doos are one- or two-passenger vehicles that are used for transportation and recreation.

Before Bombardier's invention, travel across snow-covered land was possible only by ski, snowshoe, or dog sled. The Inuit in Canada's north use the snowmobile for their daily transportation and for hunting expeditions.

Today, the original company, Bombardier Incorporated, remains the world's largest snowmobile manufacturer with plants around the world. The company has expanded and now makes other products such as **all-terrain vehicles** and airplane parts.

(opposite page, top) In Canada's Arctic, people use the snowmobile in the same way that automobiles are used in the rest of Canada. Shopping, visiting friends, and even going to church are all "doo-able" on this nifty machine.

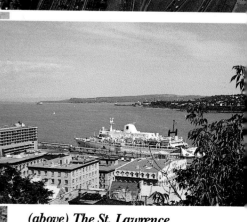

(left) Taking the train is still a popular way to see Canada.
(below) A busy highway

(above) The St. Lawrence Seaway at Quebec City

🍁 National parks and wildlife 🍁

Canada is famous for its vast areas of unspoiled wilderness. In many places, land has been set aside by the government to protect the natural environment. These areas, called **national parks**, are great places to visit and learn about nature.

Canada has 34 national parks, and more are being planned. In addition, each province has many provincial parks. Hunting, mining, and logging are forbidden in these locations. If you put all of Canada's national parks together, they would cover an area larger than England!

Endangered species

With its many protected parks and different habitats, Canada is home to thousands of wildlife species. Unfortunately, some Canadian plants and animals have become endangered due to over-hunting and the destruction of their ecosystem.

(above) At one time sea otters were almost extinct. Today their ocean habitat is threatened by pollution.

Wildlife protectors

A number of conservation groups are working with the government to address the problems that threaten Canadian wildlife populations. Laws restricting hunting and trapping have saved several species from extinction. Other problems that affect endangered animals, such as pollution and the growth of big cities, are not as easy to solve.

The first Canadian national park

The history of Canada's national-park system dates back to the early 1880s when the railroad was being built through the Rocky Mountains. Some of the workers discovered a hot spring a short distance from their camp. After soaking in the warm water for a while, they returned and told their friends.

Realizing that the spring might be valuable in the future, several people claimed ownership of the land around it. When asked to choose who would own the land, the government made the decision to preserve it for all Canadians. As a result of the tug-of-war, Banff National Park was created.

(above) The moose is a famous Canadian animal. (below left) Although western cougars are still common, the eastern cougar is now believed to be extinct. (below right) Blanchard's cricket frog is an endangered amphibian whose habitat on Ontario's Point Pelee is now protected as a national park.

Canadians are proud of the natural beauty of their country. Unfortunately, there are serious threats facing the Canadian environment. If people do not act now to correct these problems, the land will be damaged forever!

Wasting energy

Canadians use more energy per person than any other people in the world. Using a lot of energy causes pollution and wastes natural resources. Even people who live in countries with cold climates, such as Denmark, Finland, and Norway, use less energy than Canadians. Canadians are working hard to change their wasteful habits.

Air pollution and acid rain

Cars, factories, and power stations in Canada and the United States release harmful gases into the air. Big cities such as Toronto, Vancouver, and Montreal are often covered in smog. Air pollution is unhealthy to breathe and contributes to **global warming**. It also mixes with droplets of water and falls to the earth in the form of **acid rain**. Acid rain damages lakes, trees, land, and wildlife. Reducing air pollution is the only solution. The federal and provincial governments of Canada have passed laws to control the amount of harmful gases released into the air.

Damming rivers

Several Canadian rivers have been dammed to produce hydroelectric power. Large areas of land, some of which are important animal habitats, are flooded when dams are built. There are frequent battles between the government, power companies, and the people who want to preserve natural river areas. Did you know that when something harmful is being planned in your community, you have the right to fight the project?

Water worries

Although Canada is fortunate enough to have half the world's freshwater supply, Canadians have not cared for it very well. Almost every waterway in Canada is polluted, either by sewage or factory waste. The beaches of Lake Ontario are often closed to swimmers because the water is too dirty. The Halifax harbor is considered one of the most polluted bodies of water in Canada. The fish in some Canadian rivers are so toxic that they cannot be eaten. Even drinking water contains dangerous chemicals. Clean-up efforts are under way, but many people feel that tougher pollution-control laws are necessary.

Chemical farming

Most Canadian farmers still rely on poisonous chemical pesticides and fertilizers to produce successful crops, but environmentally friendly farms are making a comeback. Some farmers use natural pesticides and fertilizers that do not hurt the environment or the farmers. This type of farming is called **organic farming**.

Although organically grown fruits and vegetables do not look as perfect as other produce, many Canadians prefer food grown without chemicals. Not only is it good for the earth, but it is a better health choice.

Garbage, garbage, garbage

Canada is one of the leading producers of solid waste in the world. This waste is piling up at garbage-disposal sites called **landfills**. People are becoming very concerned about the pollution caused by landfills and the effect they have on the environment.

Governments across Canada have responded to the garbage problem by encouraging people to **reduce**, **reuse**, and **recycle**. In some cities and towns, people are forced to pay for the extra bags of garbage they put out for collection. Canadian families are making an effort to create less waste by composting their kitchen scraps. Some towns participate in large-scale composting programs. Garbage is separated, and the bio-degradables are turned into fertilizer.

Timber!

Many Canadian forests have been **clearcut**. This means that all the trees in an area have been cut down, leaving the land barren. Clearcutting has permanently destroyed much of Canada's wilderness. Logging companies now plant new trees where old forests have been cut down, but it is impossible to restore the original ecosystem of plants and animals. Canadians are fighting to preserve their wilderness areas.

Getting involved

To involve students in solving local problems, many Canadian schools have formed environmental clubs. Students participate in such projects as cleaning up polluted streams, raising money for local endangered animals, and planning environmental information fairs. Some clubs plant trees. What ecological contributions has your school made?

(above) This ancient forest on Vancouver Island has been destroyed by clearcutting.
(below) More and more farmers are using natural fertilizers that do not harm the environment.

♣ Canadian name game ♣

No one is absolutely sure about the origins of the name "Canada." Many people believe that it comes from a Native word meaning "village" or "place of many huts."

Many Canadian place names originated from various Native languages. Quebec is an Algonquin word for "narrow passage." In Iroquois, Ontario means "beautiful water." Yukon comes from the Athapaskan word "yu-kun-ah" meaning "great river."

Funny place names

Other place names are so unusual that they are funny. Ha! Ha! Lake, Peek-a-Boo Point, Pundeydoodles Corners, Joe Batt's Arm, and Joggin Bridge are just a few of Canada's more amusing place names. Head-Smashed-In Buffalo Jump may sound like a funny name, but it is a place where Native hunters drove bison over a cliff. Do you know of any unusual place names in your area?

Canada is home to people from all over the world. In a small town in the Yukon, called Watson Lake, the mix of nationalities is particularly visible in the signs that have been erected by visitors and residents. In the 1940s, a homesick American soldier put up a sign pointing in the direction of his distant hometown. Since then thousands of signs have been added to the sign post at Watson Lake. Can you find the name of your town among these signs?

⁕ Glossary ⁕

acid rain Rain that has become polluted by gases from factories and cars

agriculture Farming

all-terrain vehicle A vehicle with three or four wide wheels that is used for driving over uneven ground

amphibian An animal, such as a frog, that is capable of living on both land and water

archipelago A large group of islands

asphalt A black tar that, when mixed with sand or gravel, is used for paving roads

badlands A rocky region with many ridges, peaks, and gullies, formed by erosion

bio-degradable Describing something that can break down into a harmless form over time

canal lock A part of a canal in which the water level can be changed to raise or lower ships

chinook A warm, dry wind that blows down from the Rocky Mountains

clearcut To chop down every tree in an area

compost A mixture of decaying organic matter that is used as fertilizer

Coast Mountains A mountain range in the western part of British Columbia and the Yukon

duty A tax placed on imported goods

ecosystem A community of living things that are connected to one another and their environment

endangered species A group of animals or plants that is threatened with extinction

environment The surroundings in which plants, animals, or people live

extinction No longer in existence

fossil fuels Fuels such as petroleum, natural gas, or coal found deep beneath the earth

glacier A huge river of moving ice

global warming The theory that the earth is getting warmer because of pollution

Great Lakes A group of five large freshwater lakes: Lake Ontario, Lake Erie, Lake Michigan, Lake Superior, and Lake Huron

hailstones Pellets of ice that fall during a storm

hoodoo A rock formation shaped by wind and water

high-tech Describing something designed with the latest scientific advances

hot spring A place where unusually warm underground water flows out of the earth

inlet A narrow body of water leading inland from a larger body of water

Inuit Native people who live in Canada's Arctic

landfill A place where garbage is buried under and on top of layers of dirt

livestock Domestic animals such as cattle or pigs

lumber Wood that has been cut into boards

marmot A small furry mammal related to squirrels and groundhogs

meltwater Water from melting snow and ice

multicultural Of many cultures

natural resources Useful materials such as water, trees, and minerals that are found in nature

nomadic Describing a lifestyle of moving from place to place in search of food and shelter

peninsula A piece of land that juts out from a larger piece of land and is surrounded by water

pesticide A substance that is used to destroy harmful insects

prairie A large treeless plain or grassland

Prime Minister The head of Canadian government

produce Farm products such as fruits and vegetables

pulp and paper industry The industry that makes paper from trees

rainforest A dense forest that receives a great deal of rainfall

smog A mixture of smoke and fog

temperate Describing a climate that has no extreme highs or lows in its temperature

tide The regular rise and fall of water caused by the gravitational pull of the sun and moon

timber Wood suitable for building or carpentry

tundra A flat, treeless region in northern Canada

turbine A rotary engine that works like a waterwheel

urban center A city

wilderness A place undeveloped by people

♦ Index ♦

8 9 0 Printed in the USA 2 1 0 9 8